This Peppa Pig book belongs to

....

This book is based on the
TV Series 'Peppa Pig'
'Peppa Pig' is created by
Neville Astley and Mark Baker

Peppa Pig © Astley Baker Davies
Ltd/Entertainment One 2003

www.peppapig.com

Published by Ladybird Books Ltd 2012
A Penguin Company
Penguin Books Ltd, 80 Strand, London, WC2R ORL, UK
Penguin Books Australia Ltd, Camberwell, Victoria, Australia
Penguin Books (NZ), 67 Apollo Drive, Rosedale, Auckland 0632,
New Zealand (a divison of Pearson New Zealand Ltd)

001 – 10 9 8 7 6 5 4 3 2 1

Printed in China

Contents

The Train Ride 6

Cereal-Time Changes 10

Playgroup Puzzle 12

Odd Dino Out 13

Candy Cat's Hats 14

Food Fun 15

The Mail Trail 16

Musical Maze 18

Count the Veg 20

Danny's Dot-to-Dot 21

A Trip to the Moon 22

Sleepy Scene 26

Emily's Ice Creams 27

The Biggest Balloon 28

Fancy-Dress Fun 29

Monkey Match-Up 30

Madame Gazelle's Maths 31

Rhyme Time 32

Which Pig? 33

Path Through the Park 34

Peppa's Party Balloons 36

Dominoes 37

Colour the Costumes 38

Race in the Rain 39

Talent Day 40

Action Pig! 44

Space Shapes 45

Danny Dog's Day 46

Pirate Pedro 47

Fun in the Sun! 48

Danny's Dream 50

Copy the Cake 51

Princess Peppa's Pairs.............52

Bike Buddies 54

Miss Rabbit's Day Off 56

Transport Twos 60

Quick Quiz 61

Help Peppa Pig to find five presents hidden in your book. (The answers are on page 61.)

The Train Ride

Today, Madame Gazelle, Peppa and her friends are going on a train ride.

"Toot! Can I see your tickets, please?" Mr Rabbit asks them. The children wave their tickets in the air.

"Oh, no! I've lost my ticket!" Pedro cries.

"There's your ticket!" Zoe says, pointing to a ticket on the ground.

"Try not to lose it again," says Mr Rabbit, smiling at Pedro.

Choo! Choo!

"All aboard!" Miss Rabbit, the train driver, calls as the train pulls into the station. The children and Madame Gazelle jump onto the train and take their seats.

Madame Gazelle gives the children an activity sheet. They have to spot a boat, a signal box and a tunnel.

Toot! Toot!

Just then, George says, "I can see Grandad Dog!"

"Ahoy, there!" Grandad Dog calls.

"Hooray!" the children cheer, and then they tick 'boat' on their activity sheets.

"Toot! Tickets, please," Mr Rabbit arrives to check everyone's tickets.

"Oh, no! I've lost my ticket!" Pedro cries.

"There's your ticket!" Candy says, pointing to a ticket on the seat.

"Try not to lose it again," says Mr Rabbit, smiling at Pedro.

The train puffs slowly uphill. The train puffs quickly downhill. "Wheeeee!" cry the children.

Pedro doesn't feel very well, so Madame Gazelle lets him go to the front of the train. Miss Rabbit lets him wear her hat and drive the train for a bit, which makes him feel much better!

Quack!
Quack!
Quack!

"A signal box! That's on our list!" says Peppa, when the train stops at a junction.

"Hooray!" the children cheer and then they tick 'signal box' on their activity sheets.

The train stops at the junction to let Mrs Duck and her friends safely across, then it sets off again. Suddenly, it all goes dark. "Ooooh!"

"We're in a tunnel," Peppa says. "A tunnel is the last thing on our list!" The children tick 'tunnel' on their activity sheets and give a cheer, "Hooray!"

8

"Toot, toot! Last stop!" Miss Rabbit calls and the train pulls into the station.

"All change! Everybody off!" Mr Rabbit cries, waving his red flag.

The children and Madame Gazelle all jump off the train.

"But Madame Gazelle, how will we get home?" Peppa asks.

"We are home, Peppa!" Madame Gazelle tells her. The train has gone in a big circle, so they are right back where they started!

"Toot! Tickets, please," Mr Rabbit asks, one last time.

"Erm," Pedro says.

"Pedro's lost his ticket again!" Peppa cries.

"Pedro, can I have my hat back, please?" Miss Rabbit asks.

When Pedro lifts up the hat, there is his ticket! "Oh, that's where I put it," Pedro says, and everybody giggles.

Cereal-Time Changes

It's breakfast time! Can you spot six differences between the two pictures before Peppa and her family finish eating? Colour in a bowl each time you spot a change!

Colour in a bowl each time you spot a change!

Answers: 1) The clock on the wall shows a different time; 2) Daddy Pig's bowl is empty; 3) The lampshade is a different colour; 4) The saucepan is missing; 5) Danny Dog is looking through the window; 6) There is another magnet on the fridge.

Playgroup Puzzle

Peppa and her friends are having lots of fun at playgroup! Can you put the pieces in the correct places to complete the jigsaw puzzle?

Answer: 1 - d, 2 - f, 3 - c

Odd Dino Out

Peppa's little brother George loves dinosaurs! Help him spot the odd dinosaur out in each group. Circle it!

Dine-saw!

Answer: 1 – 4; 2 – 2; 3 – 3; 4 – 1

Candy Cat's Hats

Candy Cat has so many hats! Can you help her match the hats to the shadow shapes? Which hat does not have a shadow?

b

a

1

2

c

d

4

3

e

14

Food Fun

What are Peppa and her family doing on this lovely, sunny day? Copy the letters on the table into the correct boxes to crack the code!

15

The Mail Trail

Mr Zebra, the postman, needs your help to deliver lots of Christmas thank-you letters!

This is a game for two players. Take it in turns to throw two dice and move round the circle. When you land on a space with an envelope, tick it off on your player card. Keep moving round the circle until you have ticked off all your envelopes. The first player to do so is the winner!

Player 1

Player 2

  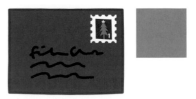

17

Musical Maze

Lead George through this musical maze until he reaches his favourite instrument, the xylophone. Pretend to play each instrument you pass along the way!

Start

Blow the horn!

Hit the piano keys!

Strum the guitar!

Count the Veg

Granny and Grandpa Pig enjoy gardening and growing lots of yummy vegetables! How many of each vegetable from the panel can you count in their garden?

Danny's Dot-to-Dot

Danny Dog is having a splashing time! Can you join the dots and add some colour to complete the picture? How many mud splashes can you count?

21

A Trip to the Moon

It is a sunny day, and George and his friend Edmund are playing with their space toys in the garden.

"Space isn't real!" Peppa tells them.
"Space *is* real, Peppa," replies Daddy Pig.
Mummy Pig tells them about a show at the museum, all about the moon. George and Edmund want to see it!

At the museum, they all buy tickets.
"Are we really going to the moon?" Peppa asks.
"No, Peppa, it's just pretend," Miss Rabbit tells her.
Mr Rabbit is the tour guide. "This way for our trip to the moon!" he calls, leading them inside. "Prepare for take-off!"

When they are all seated in the rocket, a voice booms, "Blast off!"

"We live on a planet. Does anyone know what it's called?" Mr Rabbit asks.

"The Earth?" Daddy Pig guesses.

"That's right!" Mr Rabbit smiles. "And what is the moon made of?" Mr Rabbit wants to know next.

"The moon is made of cheese, of course!" Daddy Pig jokes.

But Mr Rabbit doesn't find it very funny.

"No, the moon is made of rock. This is a serious tour, so no jokes, please!"

23

"It is _pretend_ though, isn't it?" Peppa asks when they eventually arrive at the moon.

"Yes, Peppa. If it was the real moon, you could jump over my head!" Mr Rabbit tells her. "Gravity is what keeps us on the ground, and it is weaker on the moon, so you can jump higher."

Some big rubber bands drop down and Mr Rabbit straps everyone in. Peppa and the others feel like they are jumping on the moon! It is fun!

Miss Rabbit tells them to say "Moon cheese!" as she takes a picture.

24

It is the end of the tour, so Miss Rabbit takes everyone to the moon shop.
Daddy Pig buys some moon cheese.
"I like the moon now because it's very interesting!" says Peppa, holding their
picture of them all bouncing on the moon.
"And very tasty!" laughs Daddy Pig, eating his yummy moon cheese.

Sleepy Scene

It is bedtime for Peppa and George! Tick off the objects from the panel as you spot them in the scene, before they fall asleep.

Emily's Ice Creams

Emily loves ice cream and she can't decide which is her favourite flavour! Can you colour two ice creams in strawberry pink? Can you colour one ice cream in banana yellow? Can you colour three ice creams in chocolate brown?

The Biggest Balloon

Can you help Peppa put these party balloons in order of size? Number them 1 to 5, beginning with the biggest first!

POP!

Answers: 1) melon; 2) banana; 3) pear; 4) strawberry; 5) lemon

Fancy-Dress Fun

George is having fun with his fancy dress costumes. Trace the words to match each outfit with the right type of transport!

horse

rocket

ship

Monkey Match-Up

Can you circle the monkey that matches Zoe's favourite toy?

Oooh Oooh Oooh!

Madame Gazelle's Maths

Madame Gazelle has some sums for you to solve!
Can you do the maths and add the answers?

2 + 4 =

5 - 3 =

6 + 1 =

7 - 2 =

Rhyme Time

Candy wonders if you can think of three words that rhyme with 'cat'?

cat

Write them here!

1 --

2 --

3 --

dog

Now show Danny that you can think of three words that rhyme with 'dog' too!

1 --

2 --

3 --

Which Pig?

Here is the Pig family. Can you draw a line to match each member to the correct close-up picture?

1

6

2

4

3

5

Grandpa

Granny

Mummy

Peppa

George

Daddy

Answers: Peppa - 5; George - 2; Mummy - 6; Daddy - 4; Granny - 1; Grandpa - 3

Path Through the Park

Peppa and her friends are playing in the park. Take it in turns to throw a die and race round the path, following any instructions you land on along the way. The first back to Peppa, wins!

Start / Finish

1

2

3

19

Giddy up!
Move back 2 spaces.

18

17

16

15

Splish, splash, splosh!
Move forward 3 spaces.

14

13

Flying high! Move forward 2 spaces.

4

5

6

7

Wheeeee! Move back 1 space.

8

9

10

Round and round! Miss a turn.

11

12

Bounce, bounce! Take another turn.

Peppa's Party Balloons

Peppa's found some pretty party balloons. Can you circle the odd balloon out in each group?

Dominoes

Play a fun game of dominoes with your pals! Ask a grown-up to cut out the dominoes and then divide them between the players. Take it in turns to put down a domino, making sure the picture matches the one before. If you can't match a picture, miss a turn. The first person to put down all their dominoes is the winner!

Colour the Costumes

Can you colour the picture of Princess Peppa and Sir George? Use the colour code as a guide!

Colour Key

1 2 3 4 5 6 7

Race in the Rain

Who will reach the umbrella first? To find out, follow the wiggly lines and count the muddy puddles on the way. The pig who splashes in the most puddles, wins!

Answers: Peppa – 3 puddles; George – 5 puddles; Mummy Pig – 4 puddles; Daddy Pig – 2 puddles. George splashed in the most puddles!

Talent Day

At playgroup, Madame Gazelle tells the class that tomorrow will be Talent Day.
"What is a talent?" Peppa asks.
"A talent is something you like doing and you are good at," Madame Gazelle explains.
"My talent is playing the guitar."

Just before bed, Peppa tries to decide what her talent is. "I can skip, I can sing and I can dance. It's hard to choose one talent, I am good at lots of things!"
"Don't worry, you can decide tomorrow," Daddy Pig says, tucking Peppa into bed.

The next morning, it is Talent Day. "My talents are skipping, singing and dancing," Peppa tells her best friend, Suzy Sheep. "I was practising all last night!"
"I was practising watching television last night," Suzy says.
"That's not a talent!" Peppa tells her.
"What can I do then?" Suzy wonders, a bit worried.

Danny Dog bangs the drum - loudly!
Pedro Pony does a magic trick. He
makes a glass of water disappear!
Emily Elephant plays a tune on
the recorder.

Candy Cat's talent is skipping. "I was going to do skipping, but I can still do singing and dancing!" Peppa says.
Zoe Zebra's talent is singing. "I was going to do singing, but I can still do dancing!" Peppa says.

"Suzy, what is your talent?" Madame Gazelle asks next.
"Dancing!" Suzy tells her.
Oh dear, dancing is Peppa's last talent!
"It's so nice that everyone has chosen a different talent to show the class!"

Madame Gazelle smiles. "Now Peppa, what is your talent?"
"I was going to skip or sing or dance, but they've all been done!" Peppa says sadly.
"A talent can be anything," Madame Gazelle tells her. "Think of something you really like to do!"

Peppa thinks hard. Then she cries, "I know! I've got a talent that I'm really good at!"
So everyone puts their boots on and follows Peppa outside.
"My special talent is that I'm the best in the whole world at jumping up
and down in muddy puddles!" Peppa tells the class. "Snort!"
Peppa's classmates love jumping up and down in muddy puddles too!
Everybody loves jumping up and down in muddy puddles!

Action Pig!

George is an all-action pig! Can you draw lines to link the pictures of him to the correct words?

splashing

riding

jumping

snorting

Space Shapes

Help Spaceman George complete the space shapes by tracing your pencil over the pale blue line and then adding colour.

Danny Dog's Day

Danny has had a busy day! Can you draw the little hand on each clock, so that it shows the correct time?

At 2 o'clock Danny played football.

At 5 o'clock Danny splashed in the mud.

At 6 o'clock Danny rode his bike.

Pirate Pedro

Pirate Pedro needs your help! Can you count the coins in each row? Which row has the most coins?

a

b

c 5

d 7

Fun in the Sun!

Complete the beach scene with your summer holiday stickers!

Danny's Dream

What is Danny dreaming about tonight? Cross off all the letters that appear more than twice to reveal a word.

50

Copy the Cake

Peppa and George are having a party! Can you copy the picture of this delicious-looking chocolate cake, using the grid as a guide?

Princess Peppa's Pairs

Princess Peppa and Sir George want to play a game with you and a friend or two!

  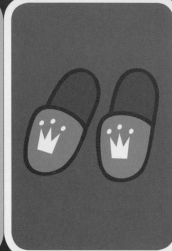 

First, cover each picture with a piece of paper. Then take it in turns to remove two pieces of paper, one from the left page and one from the right page, to see if you've picked a pair. If you have, keep the pieces of paper. If not, put them back. The player with the most pieces of paper when all the pairs have been picked is the winner!

Bike Buddies

Peppa and her friends are having lots of fun on their bicycles. Use your coloured pens or pencils to carefully trace their trails!

Miss Rabbit's Day Off

Last night, Peppa, George and Suzy Sheep had a sleepover at Rebecca Rabbit's house. This morning, they all eat yummy carrots for breakfast, then Daddy Rabbit goes off to work.

"Why don't you work, Mummy Rabbit?" Suzy asks. "I do work, Suzy! Who do you think looks after these two little bunnies?" Mummy Rabbit tells her.

Just then, Mummy Rabbit's sister, Miss Rabbit, stops by. "I can't stay long, I've got lots of work to do. I work at the supermarket checkout, on the ice-cream stall and driving the bus," she tells them.

But when she goes to leave, Miss Rabbit trips over a toy. Oh, no! She has hurt her ankle and can only hop! Mummy Rabbit tells her to stay with the children at home and rest, and says she will do the work instead.

The supermarket is first. Mummy Rabbit has never worked on a checkout before. The customers ask her lots of questions and she doesn't know the answers!

Back at home, Suzy dresses up in her nurse's uniform. She tells Miss Rabbit to stick out her tongue and say "Aaaah!"

Then the phone rings. Peppa answers it and it is Mummy Rabbit. "This job is going to take me all day!" she says. "We're going to need some more help."

Peppa phones the ice-cream stall. Daddy Pig is waiting at the stall and he answers the phone. "Daddy, Miss Rabbit is ill. You have to sell the ice cream today!" Peppa tells him. "I'm an expert in ice cream!" Daddy Pig says. But he finds that all the ice cream has melted, so he serves ice-cream soup instead!

Next, Peppa phones Granddad Dog. "Granddad Dog, Miss Rabbit is ill. Can you drive the bus today?" she asks.
"Of course, Peppa," Granddad Dog says. "All aboard!" he calls as he climbs out of his pick-up truck and onto the bus.
But just as Granddad Dog starts driving, Mummy Sheep phones him. Her car has broken down! Granddad Dog has to drive the bus backwards to fix Mummy Sheep's car.

Granddad Dog finds that driving a bus is quite hard.
Daddy Pig finds that selling ice cream is quite hard.
Mummy Rabbit finds that running a supermarket checkout is quite hard.

At the end of the day, they are all glad to go home. "Are you feeling better?
You will be back to work tomorrow, won't you?" they ask Miss Rabbit. "It's not
easy doing all your jobs!"
"It's not easy looking after your little bunnies either!" Miss Rabbit laughs.
They will all be back doing their own jobs tomorrow!

Transport Twos

Daddy Pig loves to take trips in the car! Can you draw lines to match these other vehicles into pairs? Which one is not part of a pair?

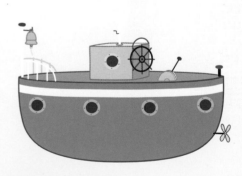

Quick Quiz

It's nearly time to wave bye to Peppa! But before you do, are you able to answer these six questions about your favourite pig and her family and friends?

1

How many pigs are in Peppa's family?

2

What noise does Peppa make?

3

Who is Peppa's best friend?

4

What is Peppa's little brother called?

5

Who teaches Peppa and her friends at playgroup?

6

What messy thing does Peppa love doing best?

Did you find five presents in your book? The presents are hidden on pages: 21, 23, 26, 47 and 52

Answers: 1) 6 pigs; 2) A loud snorting noise; 3) Suzy Sheep; 4) George; 5) Madame Gazelle; 6) Jumping up and down in muddy puddles.